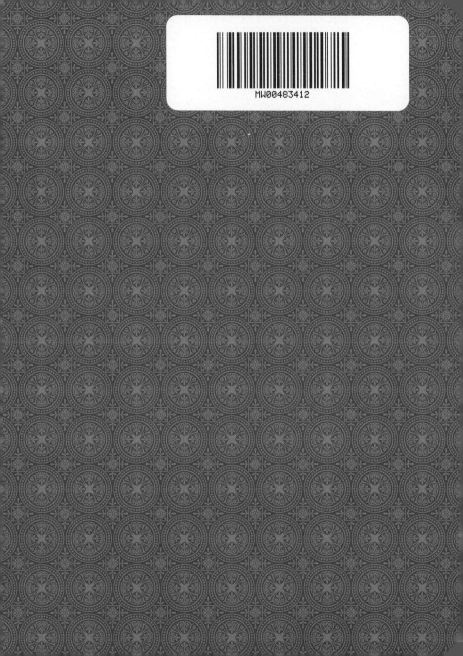

MW00483412

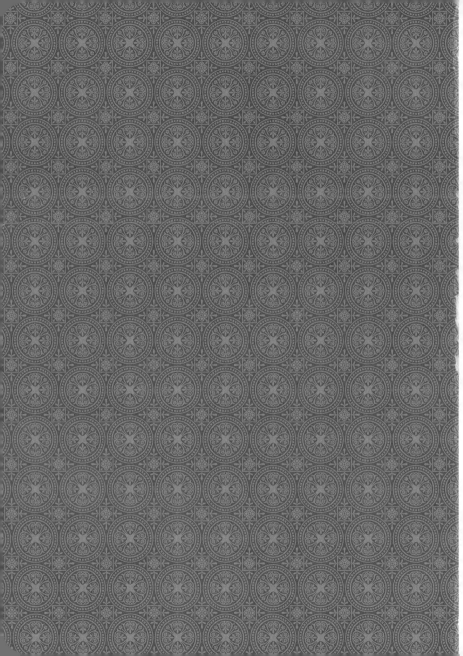

The LORD taketh pleasure in them that
fear Him, in those that hope in His mercy.
~ Psalm 147:11

For the LORD is good; His mercy is everlasting;
and His truth endureth to all generations.

~ Psalm 100:5

The joy of the LORD is your strength.
Nehemiah 8:10

To

From

Date